THE WORLD'S MOST DIFFICULT MAZE

Dave Phillips

Dover Publications, Inc.
New York

FOREWORD

A maze is a confusing system of pathways. A maze traveler is one who enters a maze in the hope of solving it. But why should anyone want to plunge into a prison of eluding pathways, pathways with the sole purpose of getting you lost? People throughout history have treated themselves to bewildering journeys through silent, immovable walls of hedges, or mazes of solid paper and ink. Is it simply the challenge; something to idle away the time? Whatever the reason for the fascination with mazes, I would not reveal it, even if I knew the secret. I am a maze maker, and I have created the maze you hold. The walls are impenetrable black lines, which you may not cross. I have used every devious trick I could contrive to keep you from the solution. I have not been kind. If you have that obscure fascination for mazes, this book is for you. You may even solve it—some day.

Published in Canada by General Publishing Company, Ltd., 30 Lesmill Road, Don Mills, Toronto, Ontario.
Published in the United Kingdom by Constable and Company, Ltd., 10 Orange Street, London WC2H 7EG.

The World's Most Difficult Maze is a new work, first published by Dover Publications, Inc., in 1980.

International Standard Book Number: 0-486-23970-5
Library of Congress Catalog Card Number: 80-68091

Manufactured in the United States of America
Dover Publications, Inc.
180 Varick Street
New York, N.Y. 10014

INSTRUCTIONS

This book contains one maze. Start is the large hexagon on the first page. Finish is the large hexagon on page 31. You may travel along the pathways in any direction, as long as you do not cross a black line. When you come to a hole in the page, you can either pass through it, or go back the way you came to try another route. If you decide to pass through a hole, you will fall onto the small blank hexagon that you can see through the hole. For instance, if you pass through a hole on page 5, you will fall onto the blank hexagon directly beneath that hole, on page 7. Similarly, if you should fall through the same hole on page 6, you would end up back on page 4. Ignore and simply pass through hexagons without holes that you encounter on your journey. There are no dead-ends in this book, neither shall you ever find an area from which you cannot escape. It is possible to find the solution from any point in the maze. It is necessary to go backward at times in order to go forward again. On pages 32–48 of this book I show the shortest possible solution. The chances of *your* finding the shortest route are very slim; you will do very well to find *any* solution. I suggest that you do not use a pencil but rather roam freely through the maze, as if you were really inside it.

START

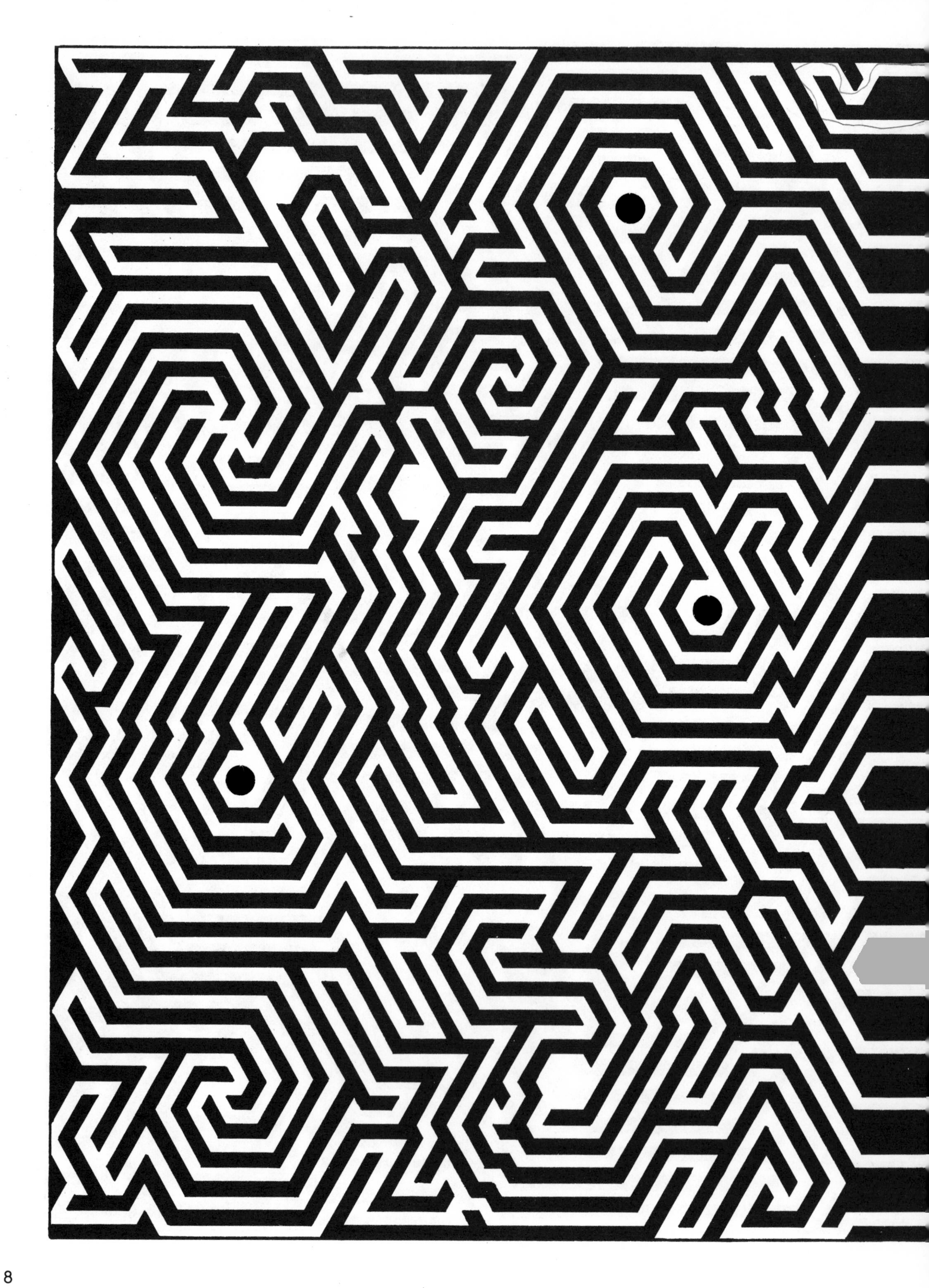

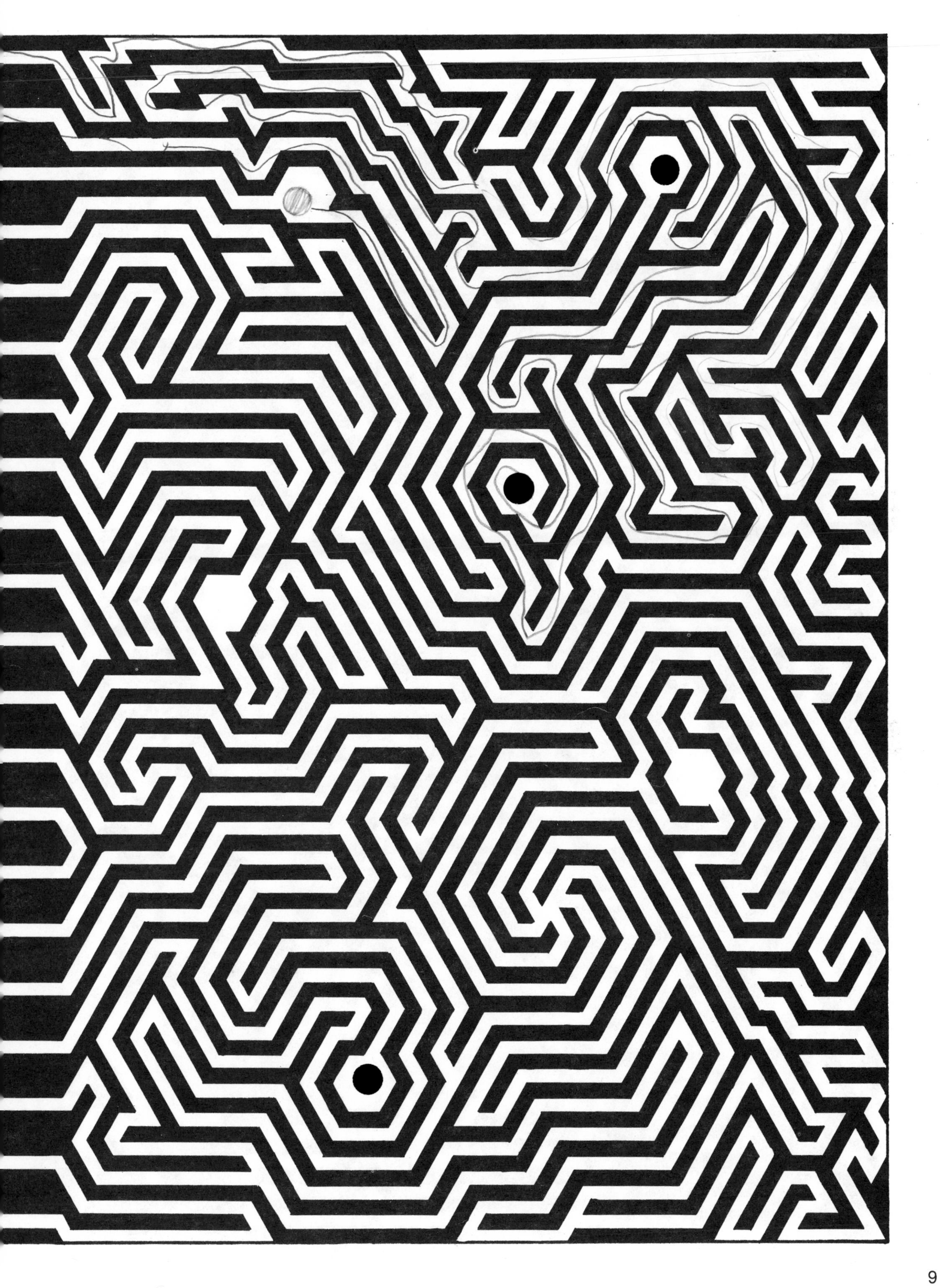

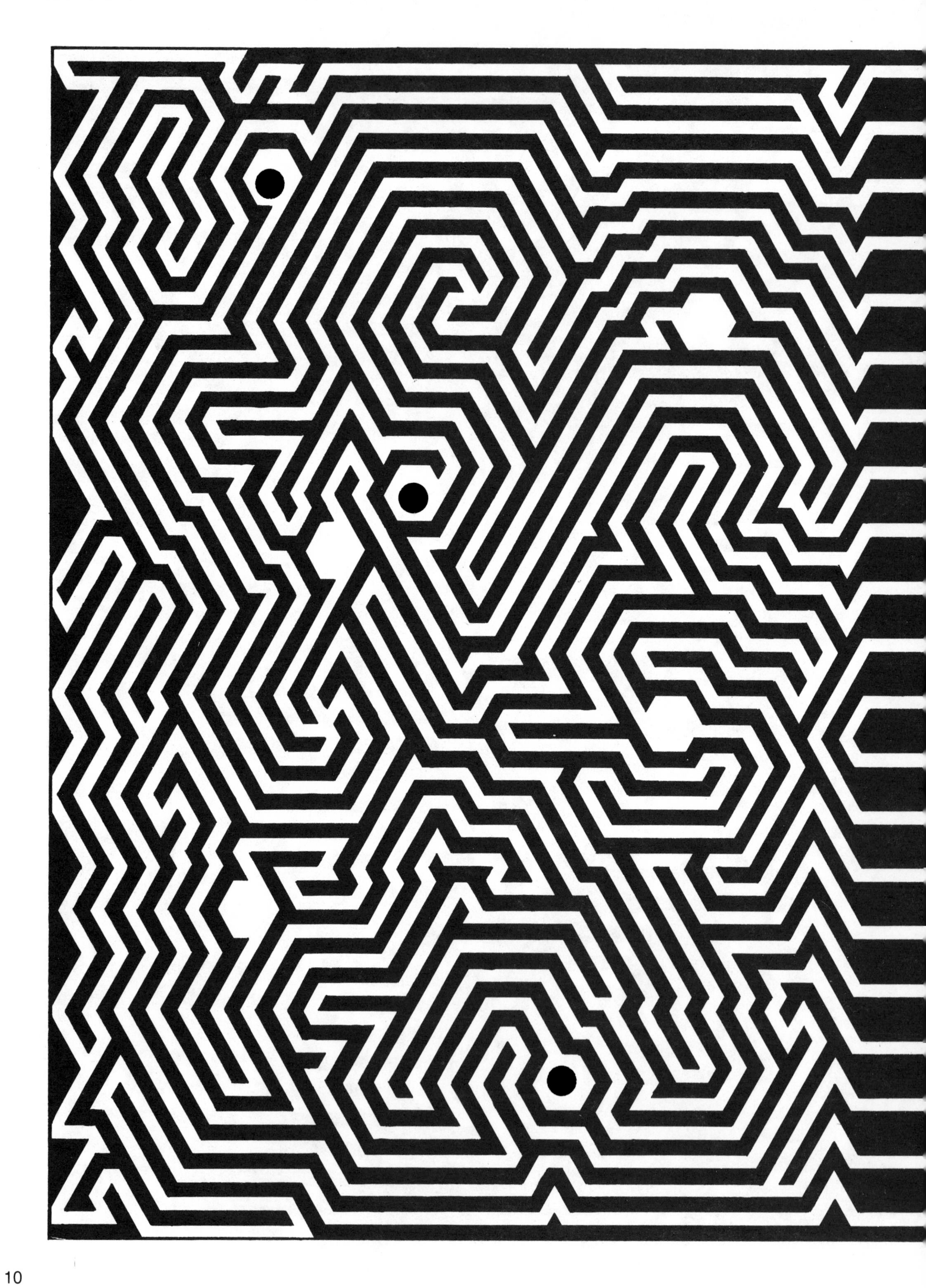

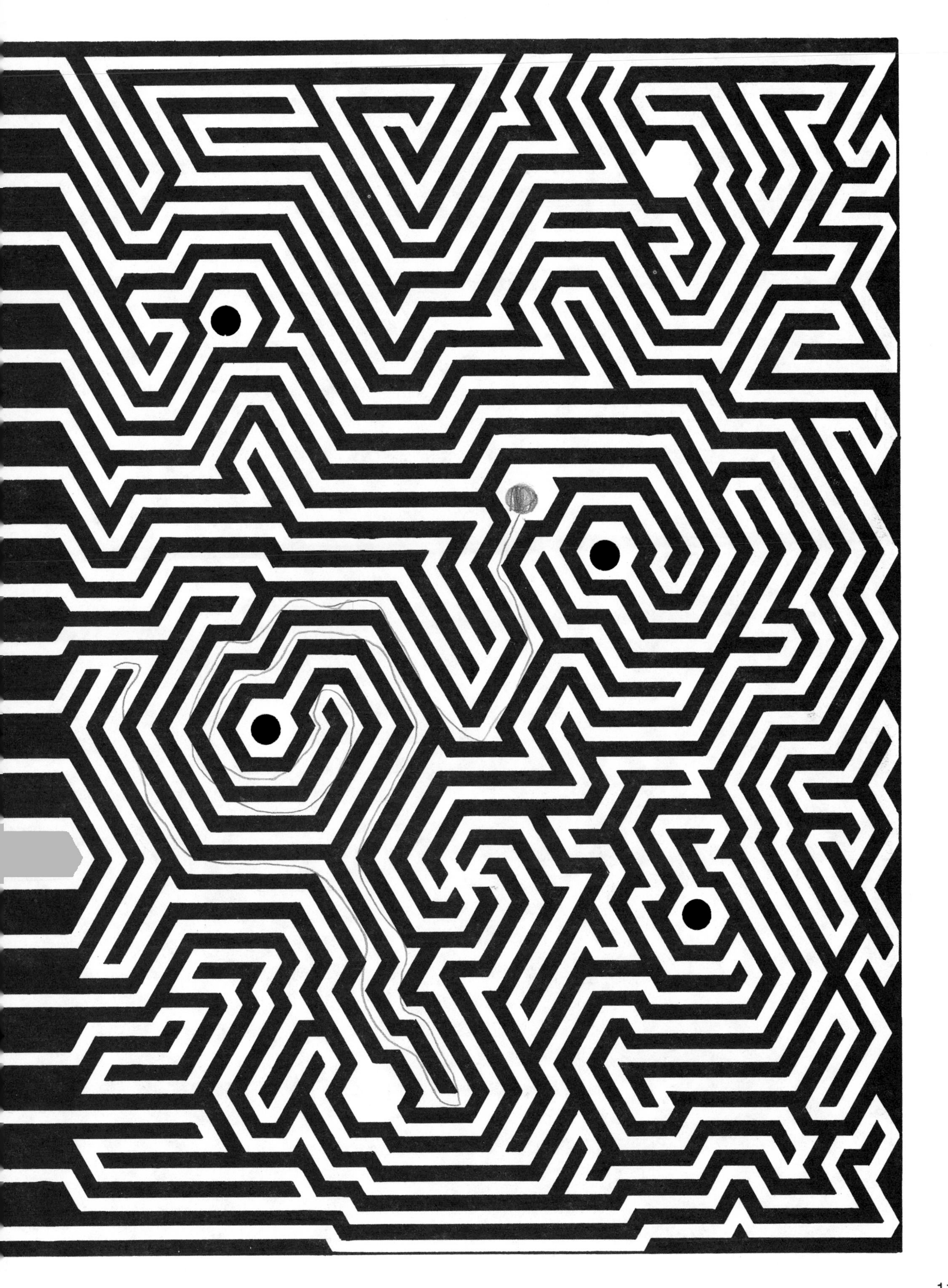

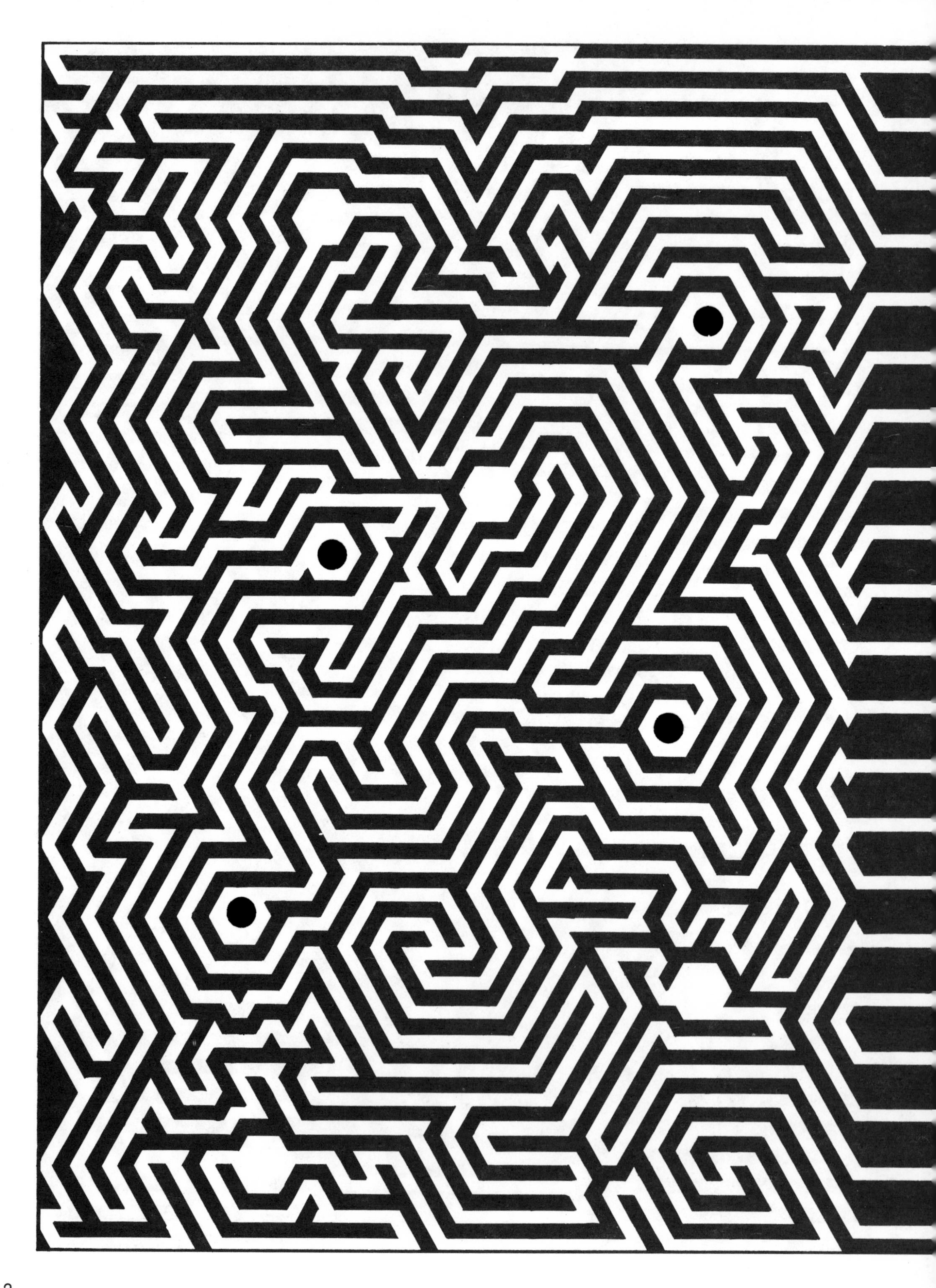

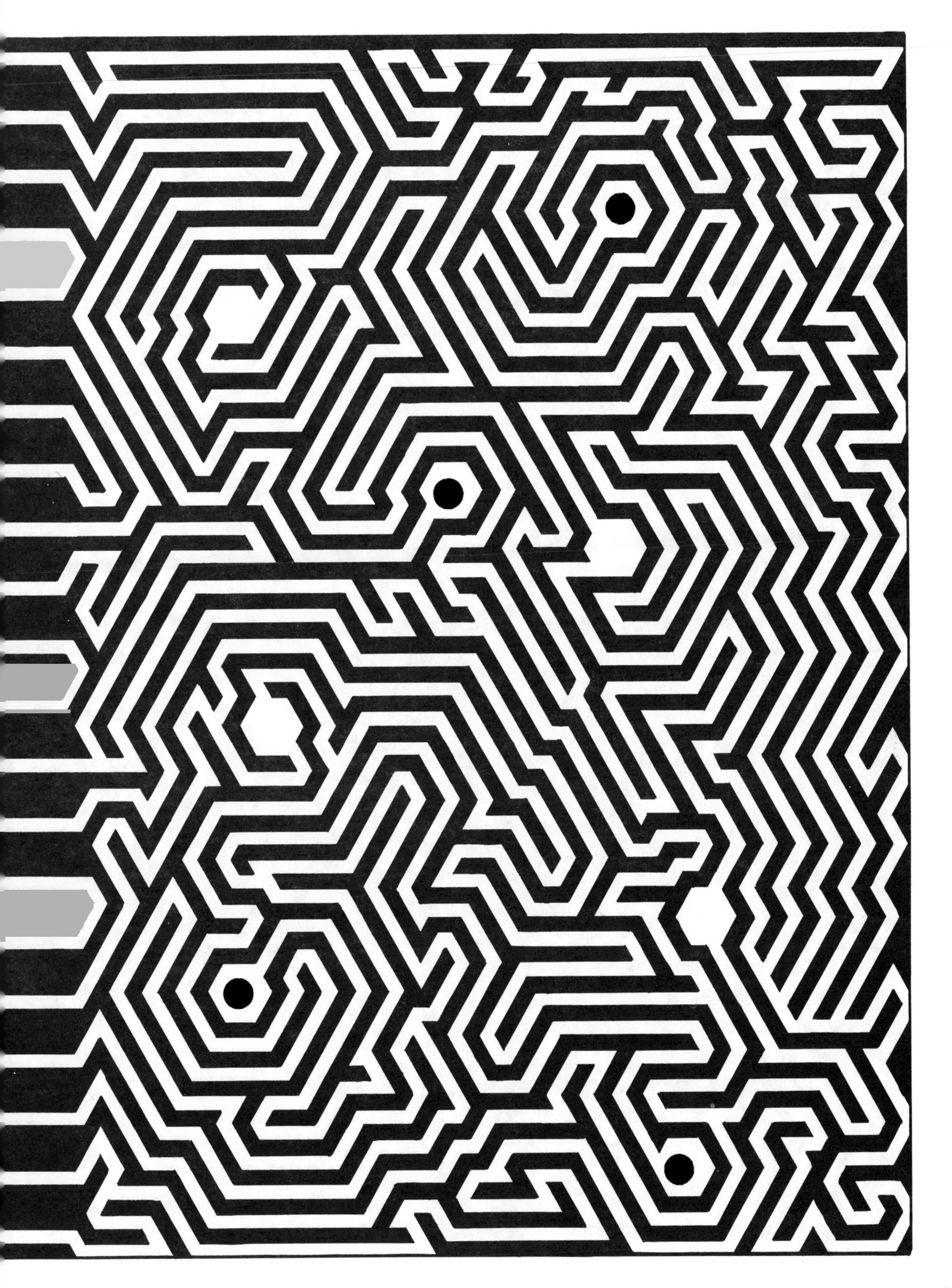

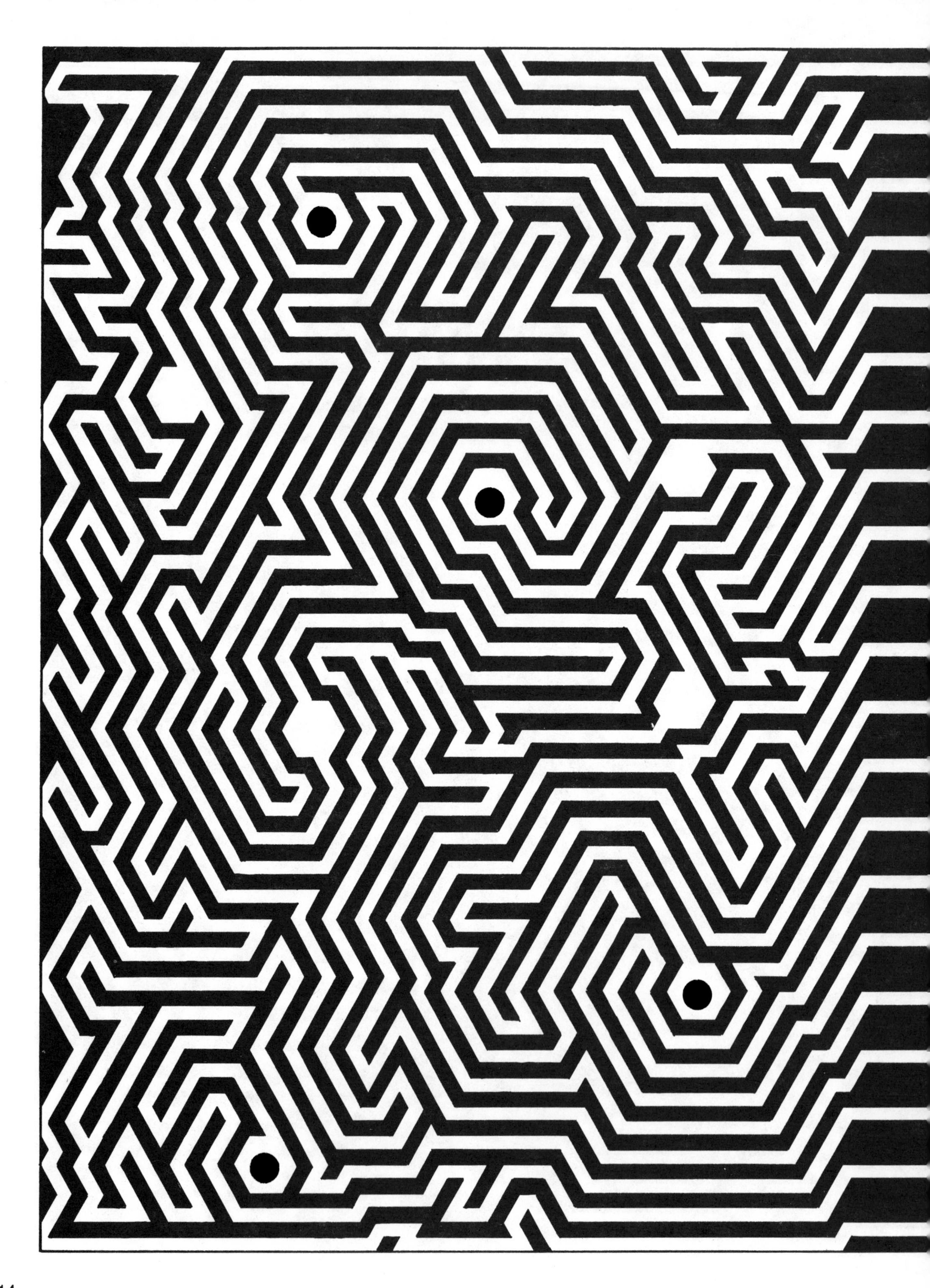

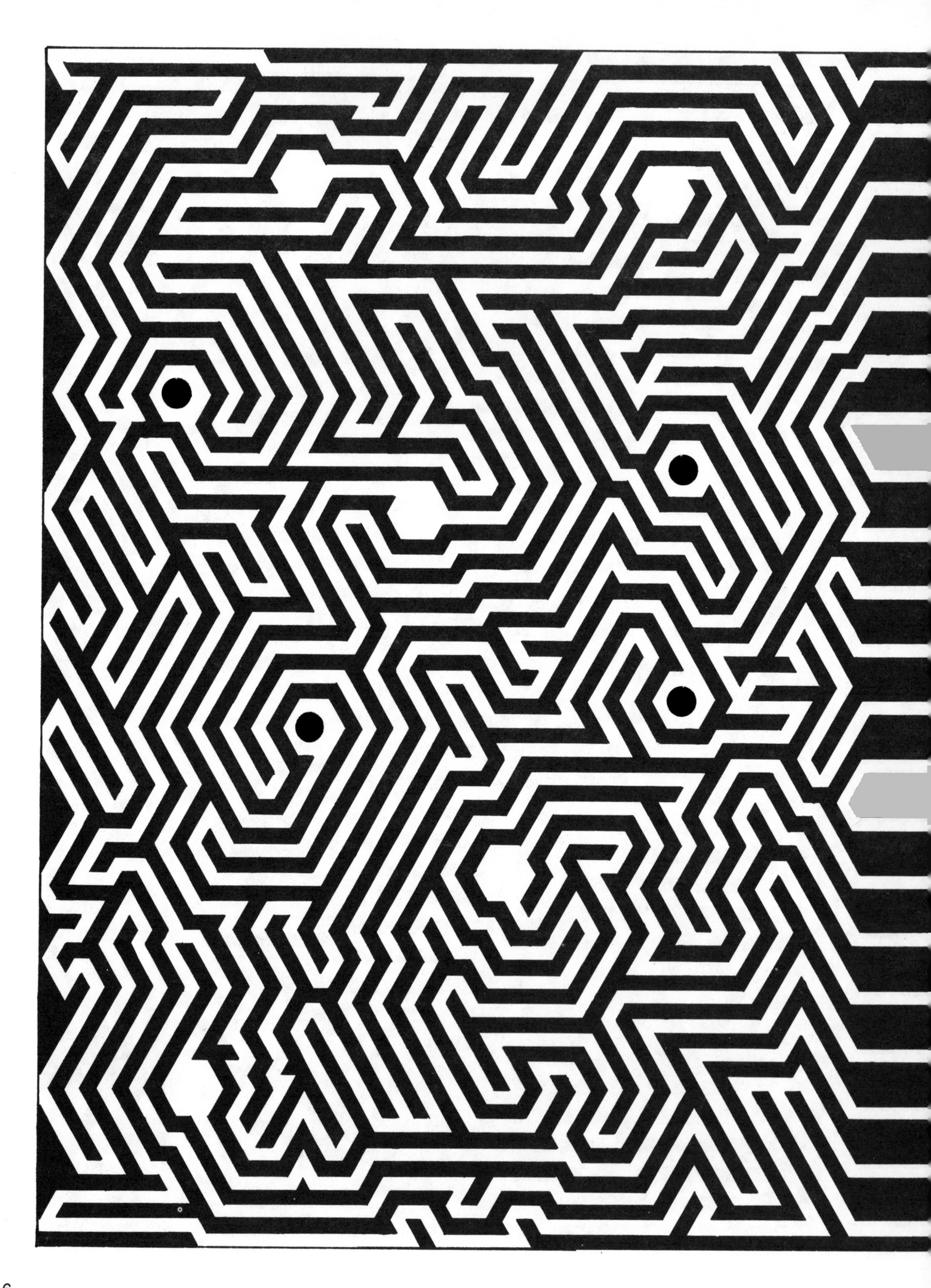

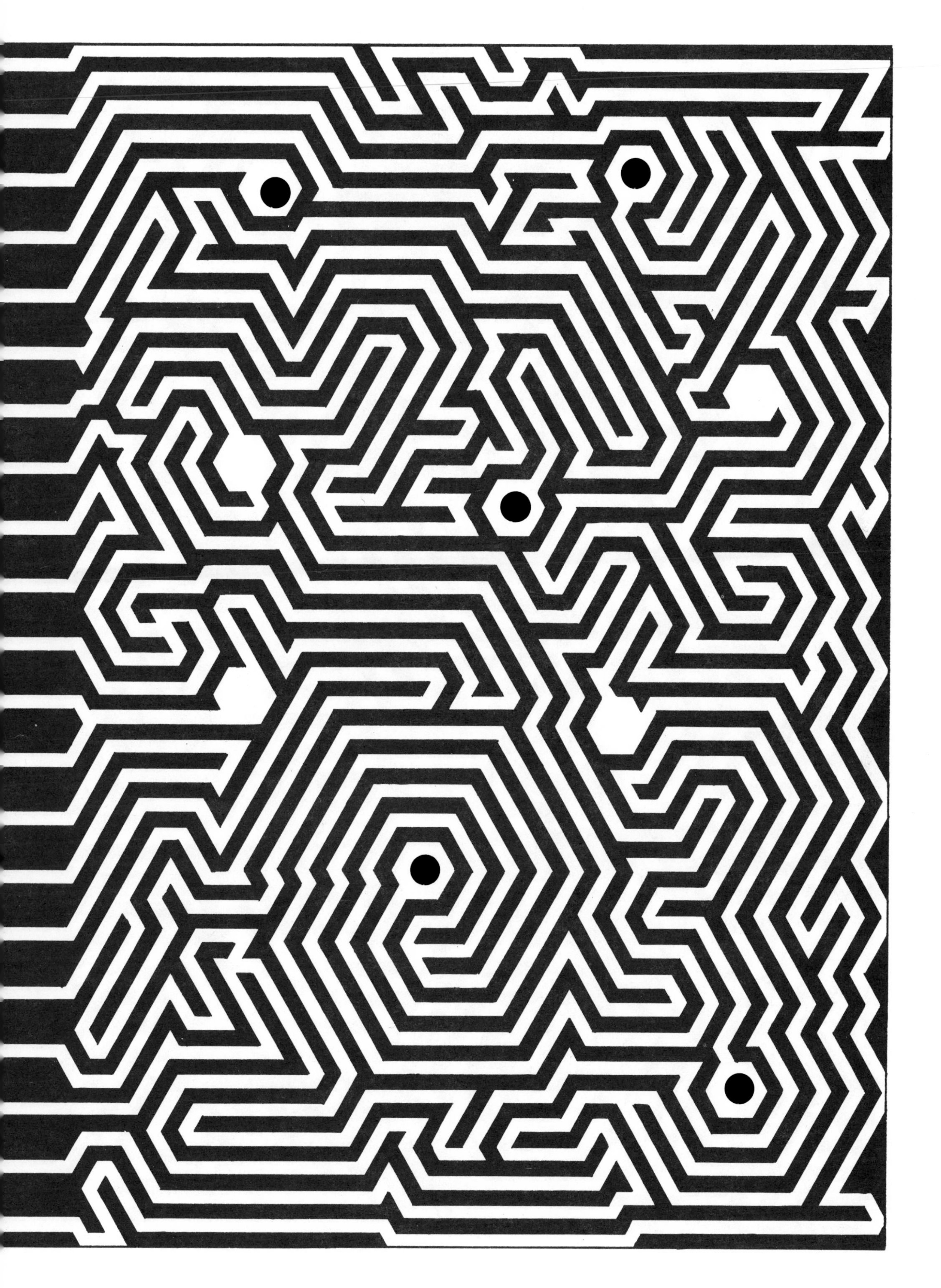

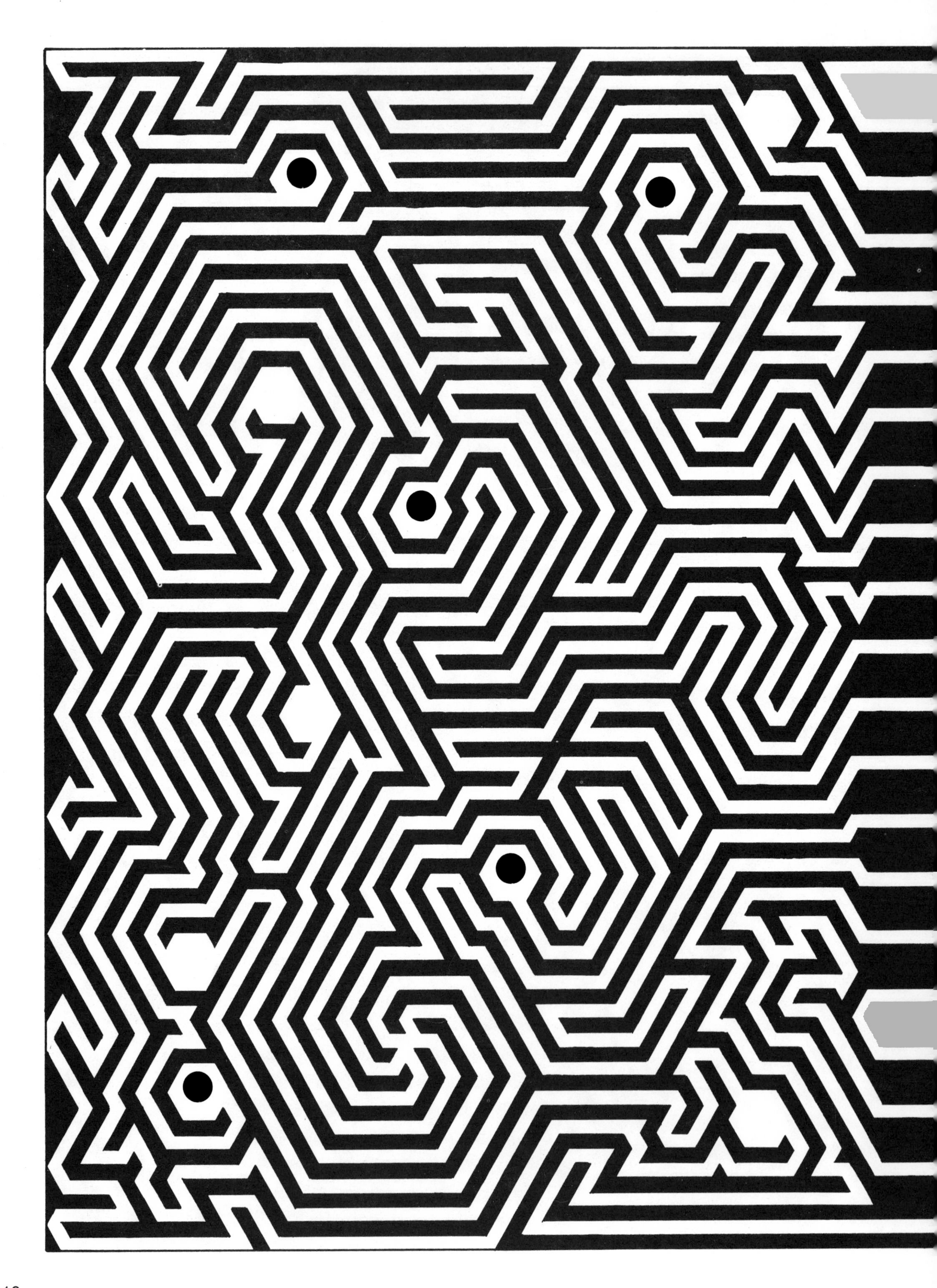

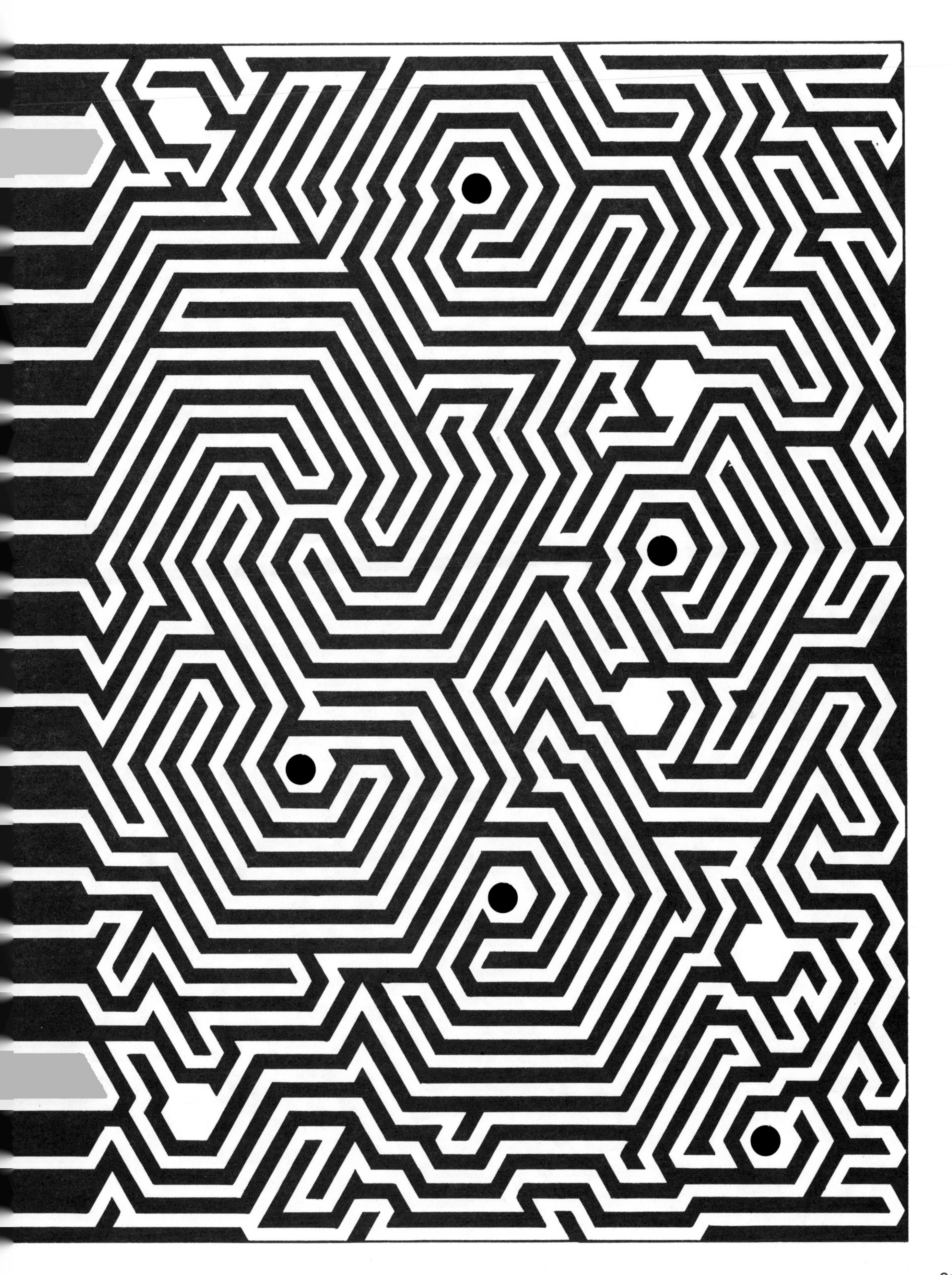

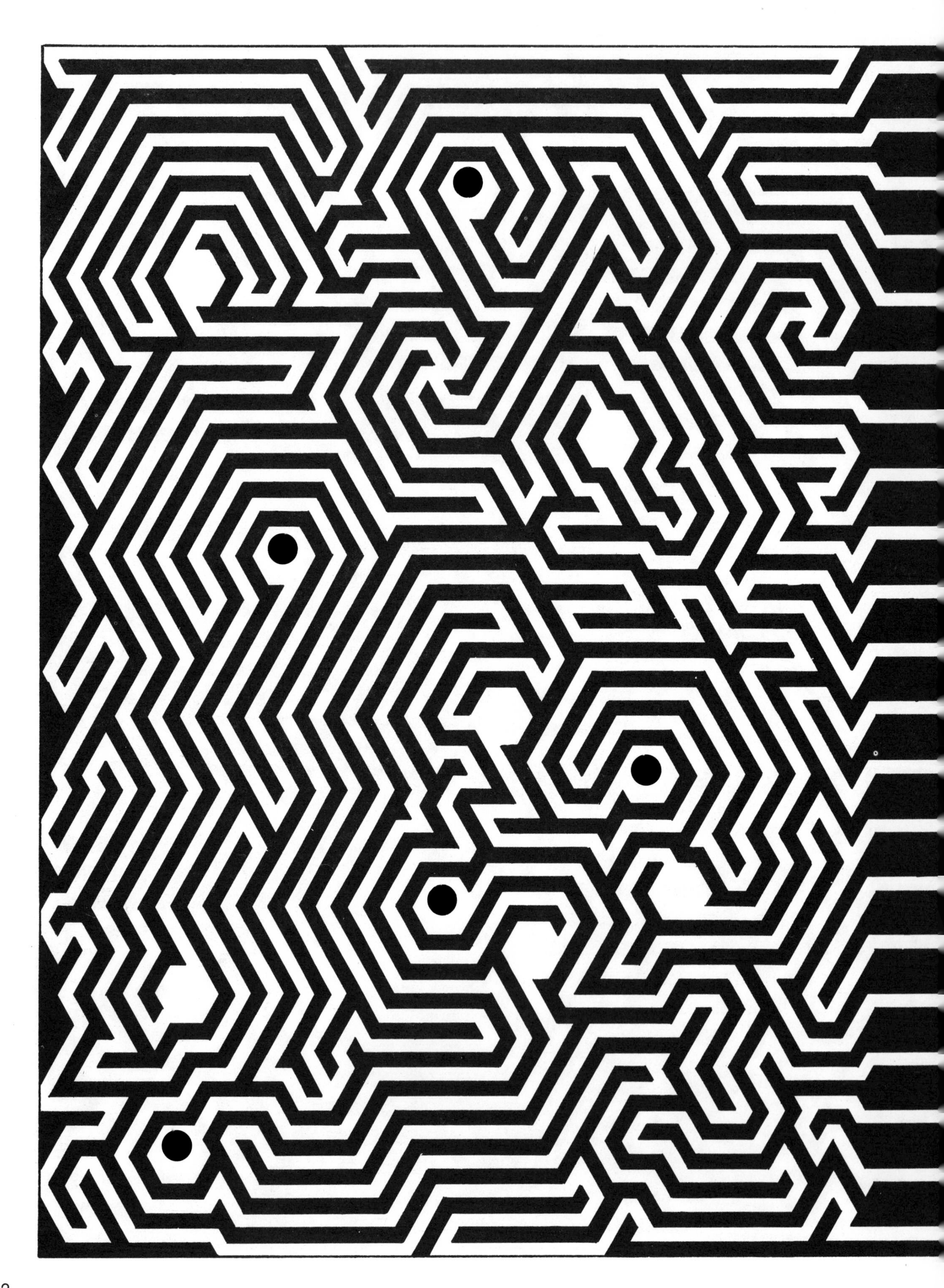

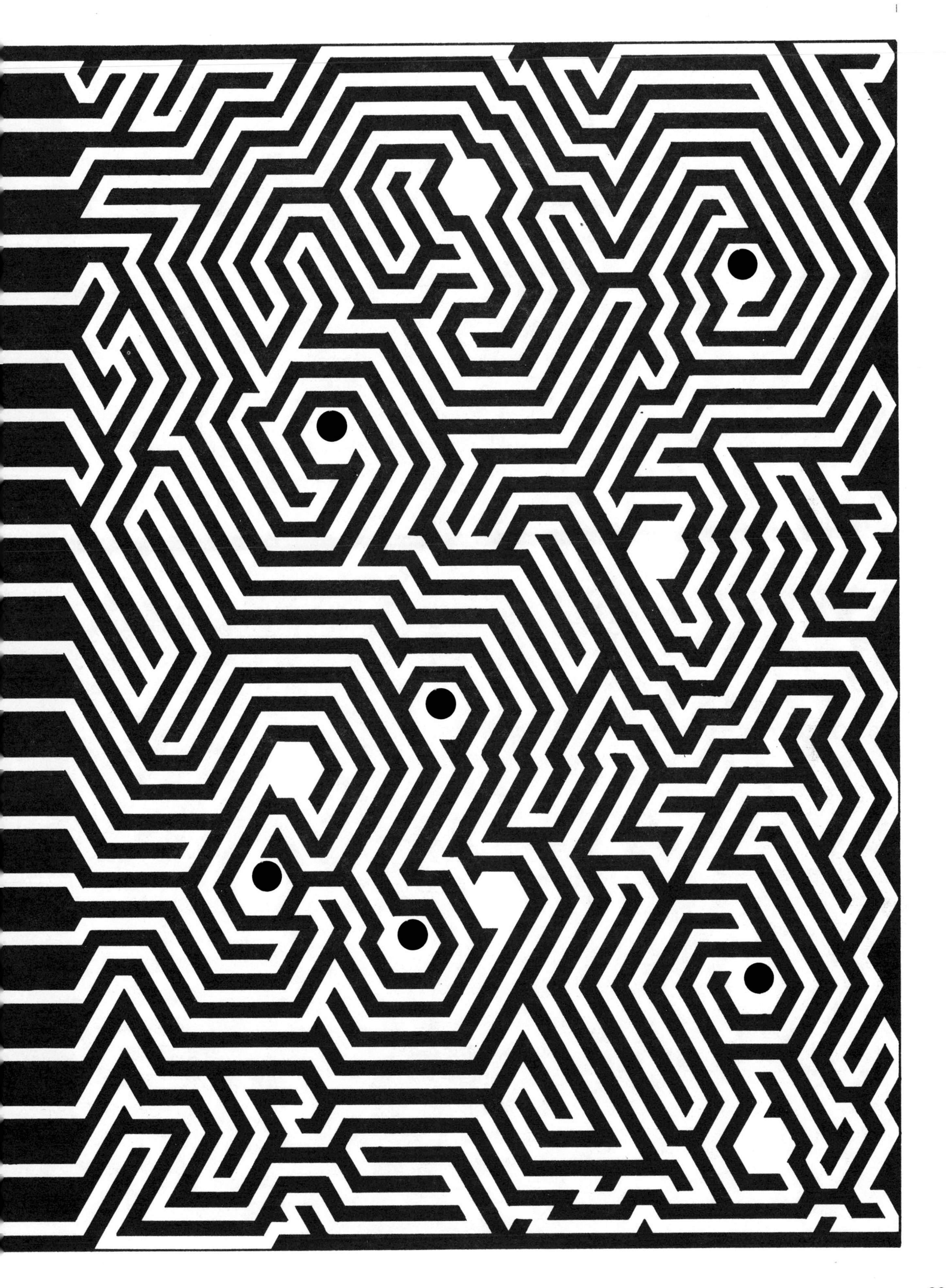

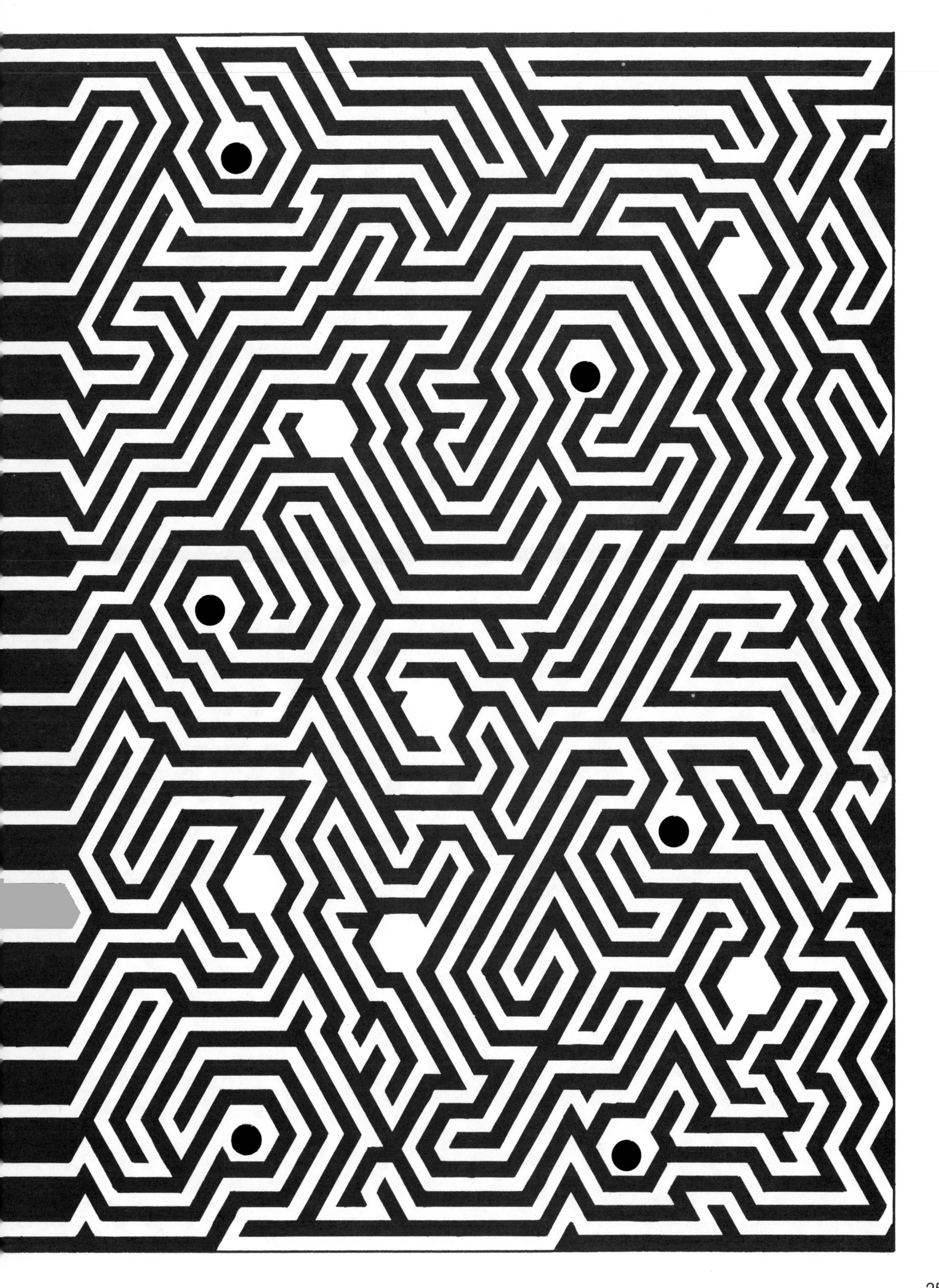

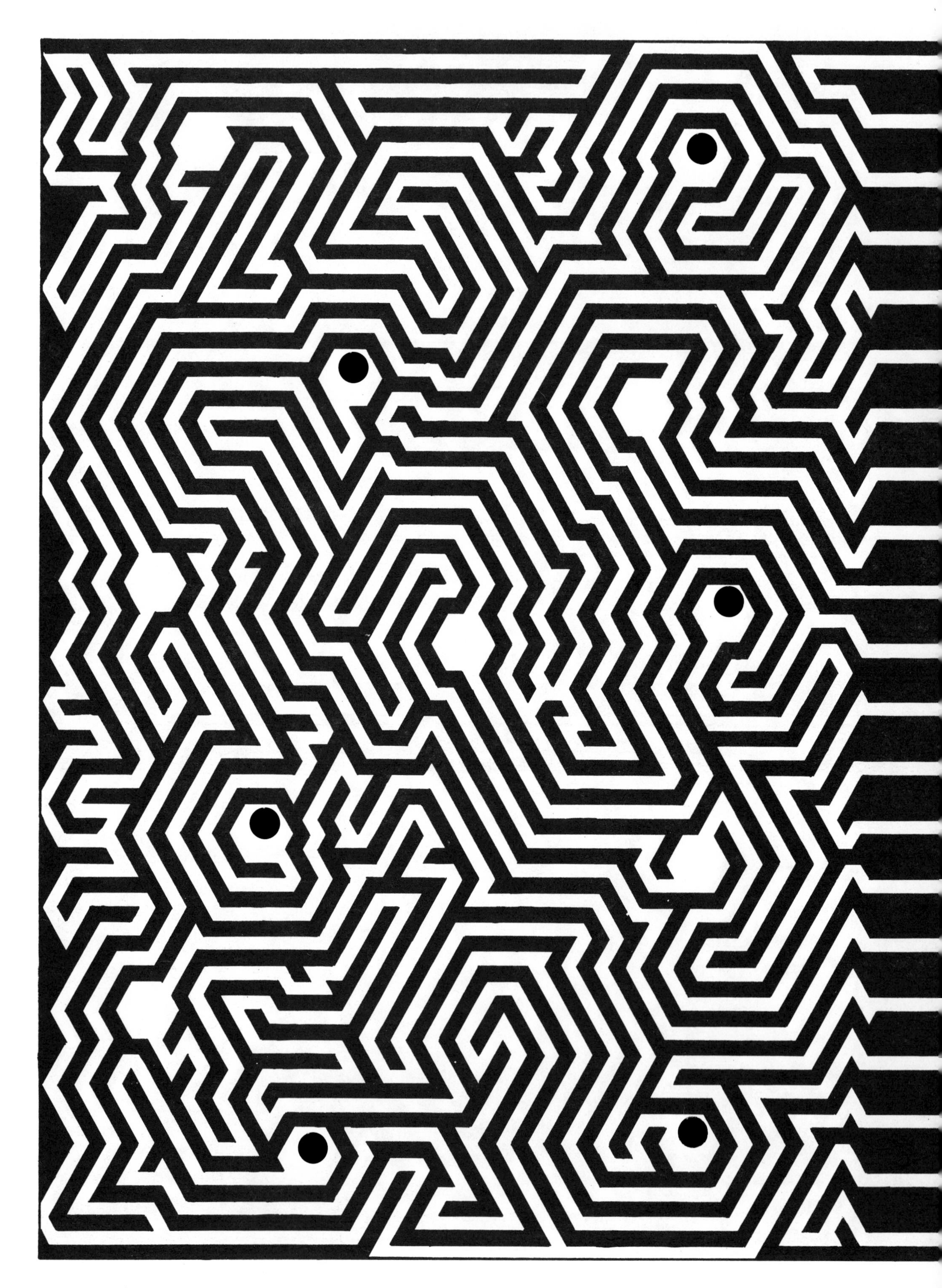

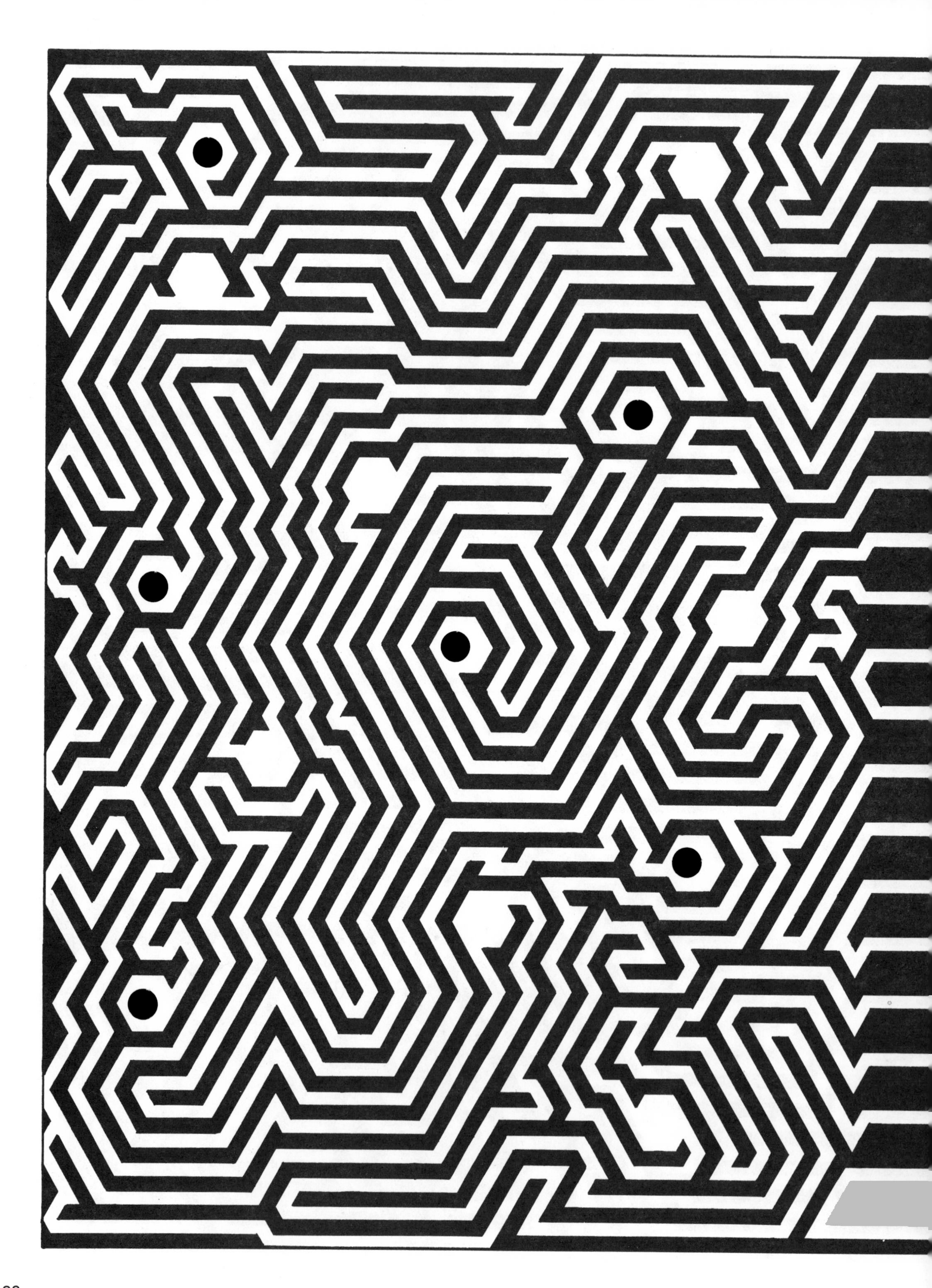

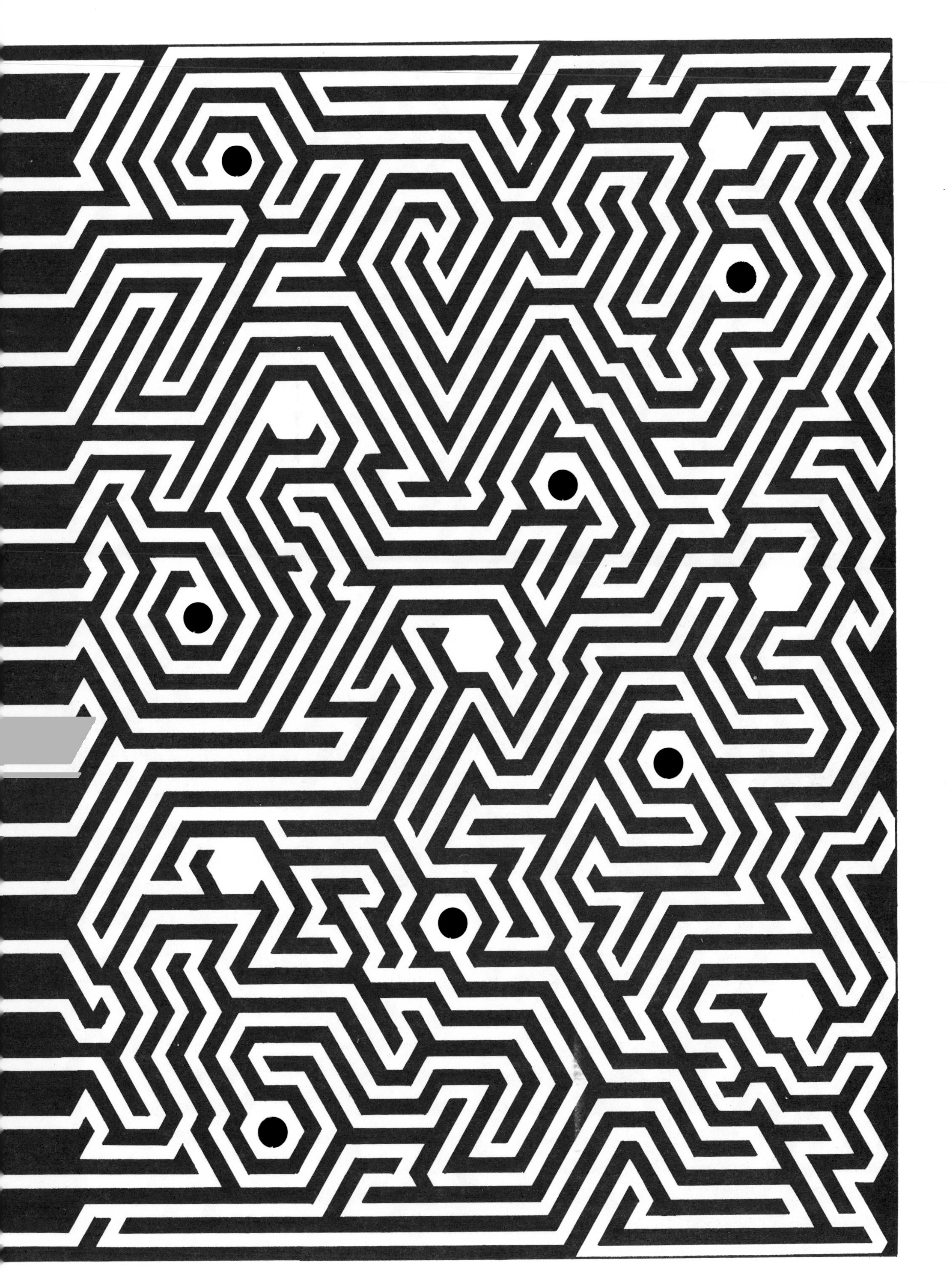

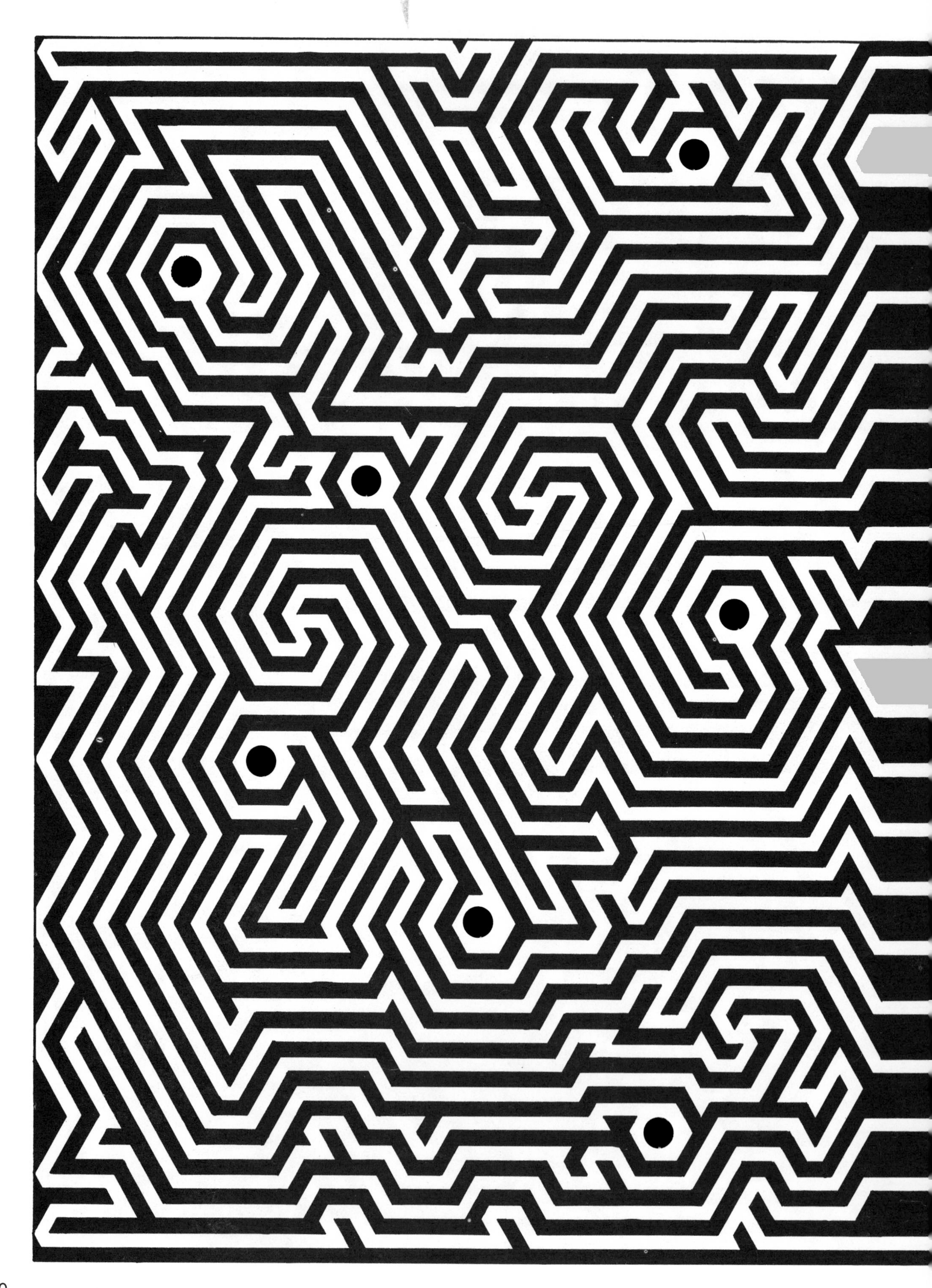

THE
END

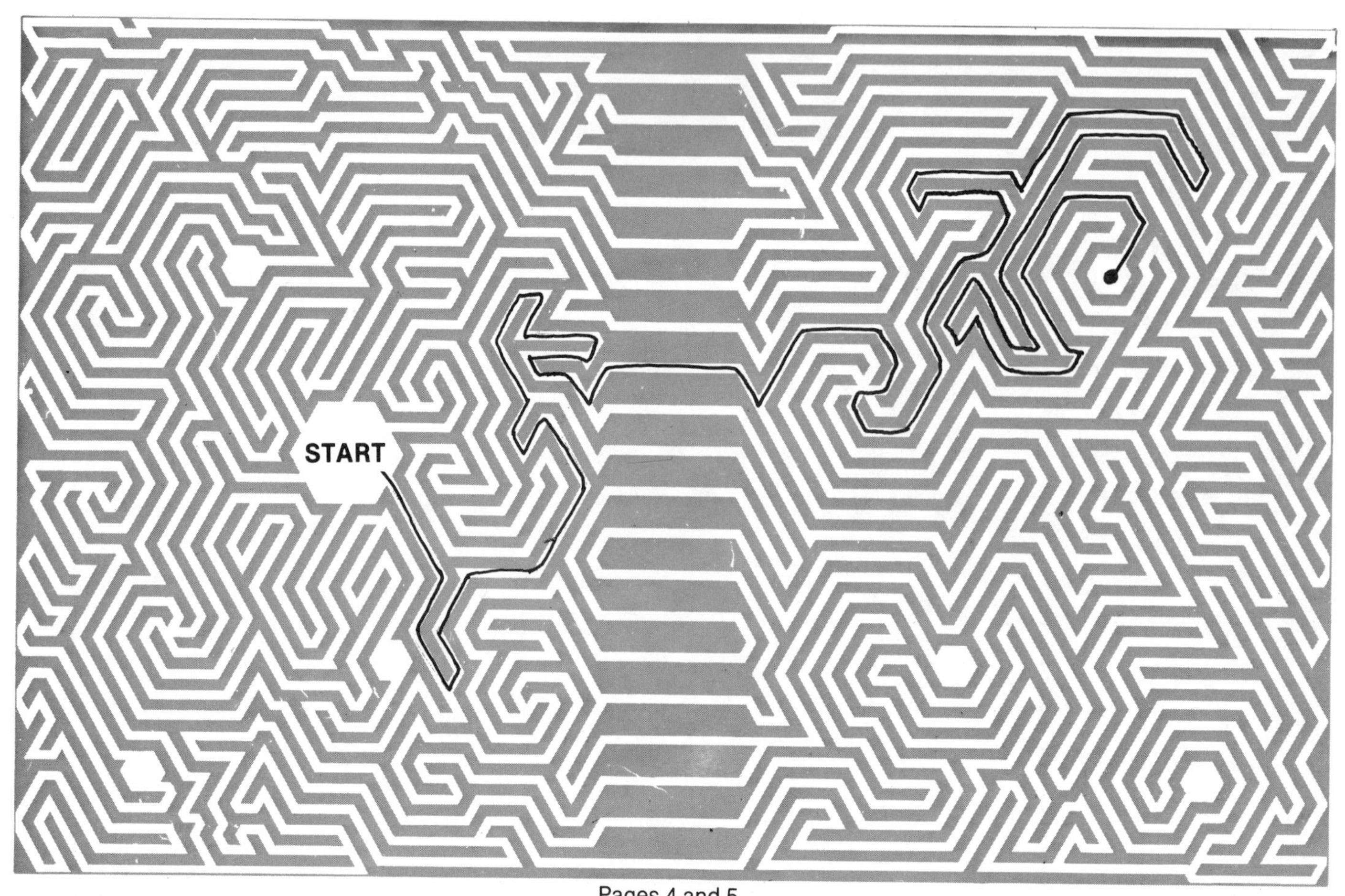

Pages 4 and 5

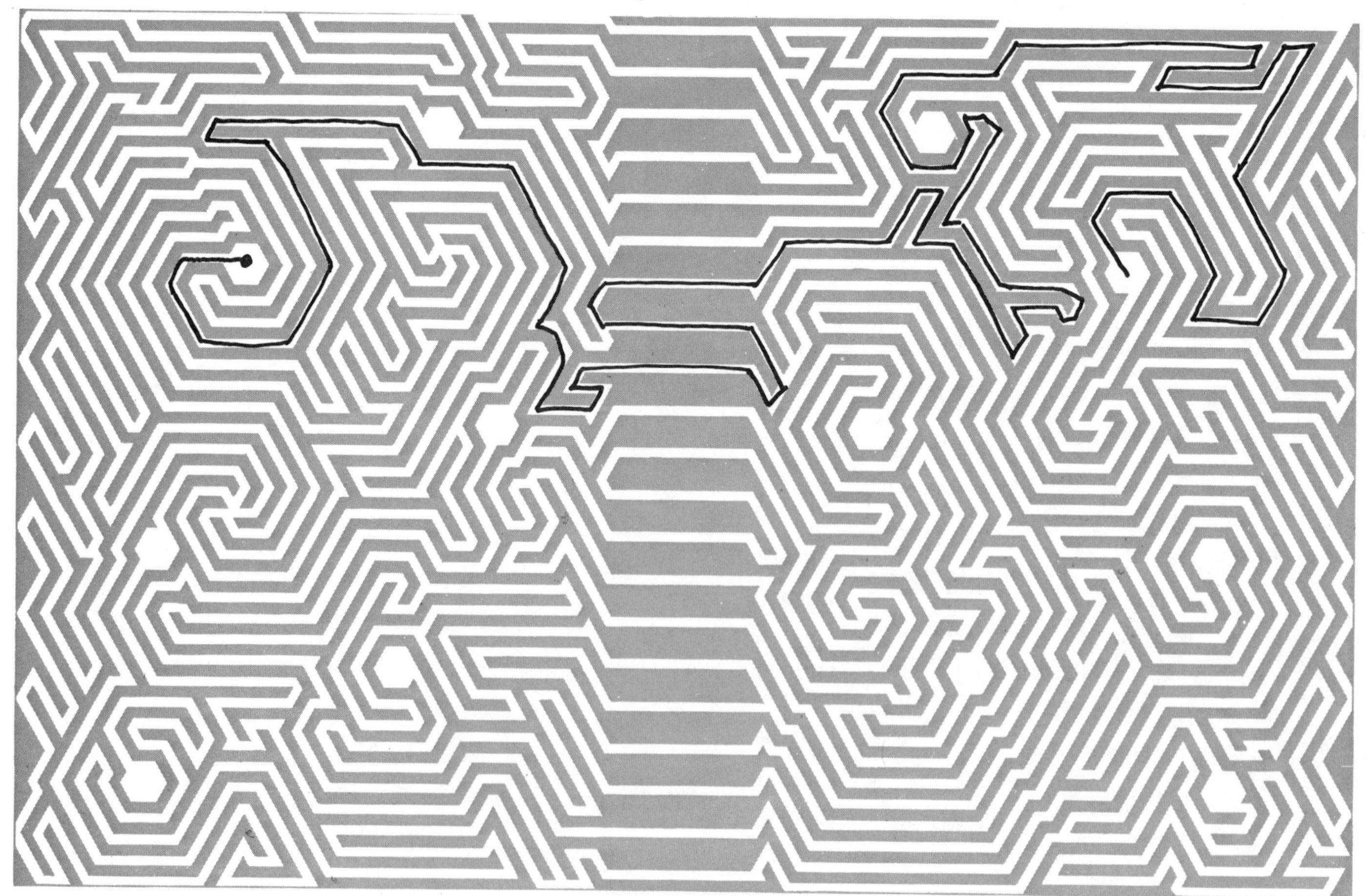

Pages 6 and 7

A small black circle in a hexagon at the end of the route on a page indicates the place at which you drop through a hole.

Pages 4 and 5

Pages 6 and 7

Pages 8 and 9

Pages 10 and 11

Pages 12 and 13

Pages 14 and 15

Pages 16 and 17

Pages 14 and 15

Pages 12 and 13

Pages 10 and 11

Pages 12 and 13

Pages 14 and 15

Pages 16 and 17

Pages 18 and 19

Pages 16 and 17

Pages 18 and 19

Pages 20 and 21

Pages 22 and 23

Pages 24 and 25

Pages 26 and 27

Pages 24 and 25

Pages 26 and 27

Pages 28 and 29

Pages 26 and 27

Pages 24 and 25

Pages 22 and 23

Pages 20 and 21

Pages 22 and 23

Pages 24 and 25

Pages 26 and 27

Pages 28 and 29

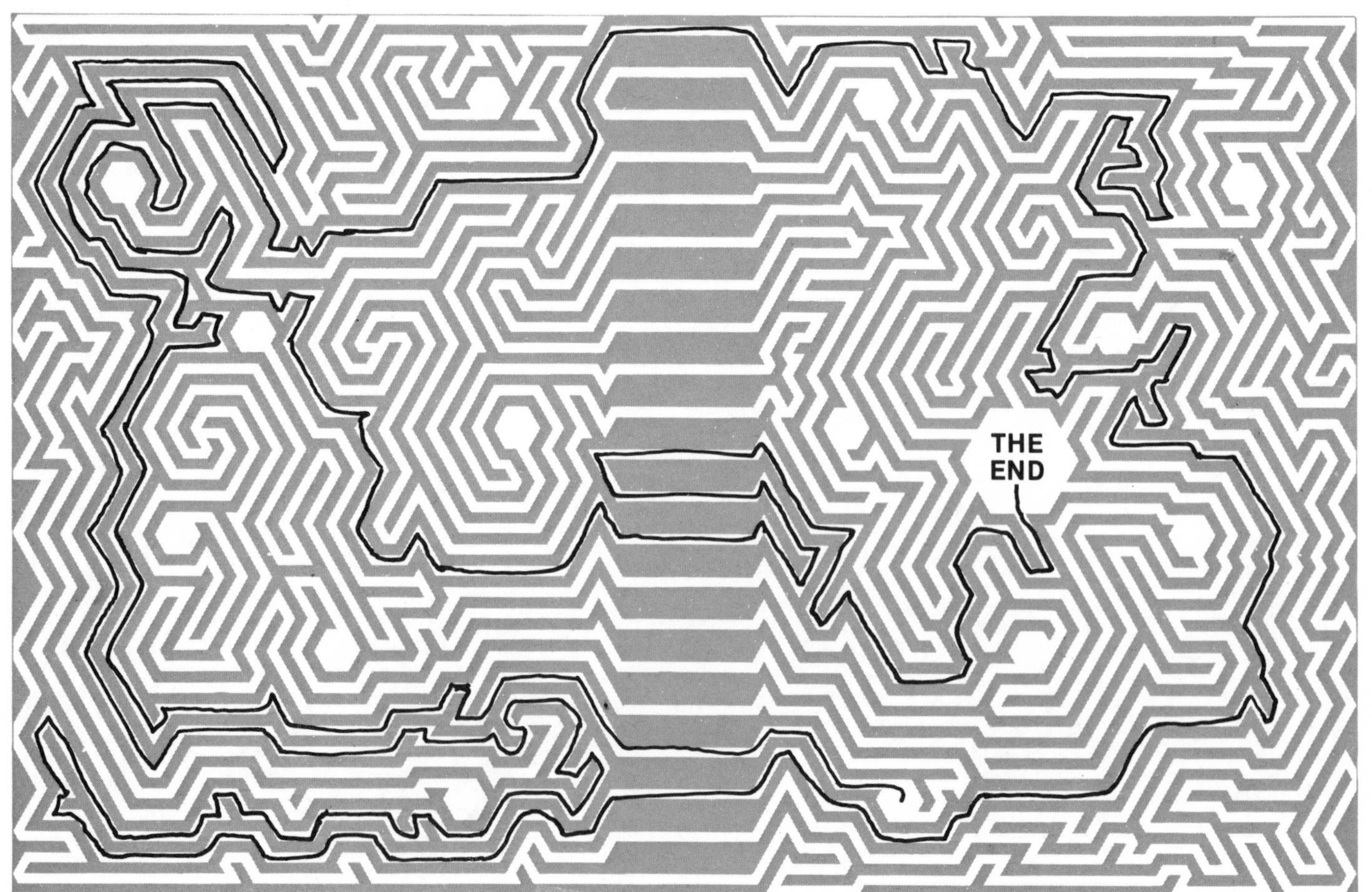

Pages 30 and 31